Revival Keys

The greatest and most urgent of all our needs
Is a revival of true godliness!
Become a revival agent—today...

Nine Challenging Bible Searches
Practical Suggestions
Supplemental Resources
Everything You Need To Begin!

WWW.FASTMISSIONS.COM

Copyright © 2022 by Dan Vis
All rights reserved
including the right of reproduction
in whole or in part in any form.

All Scripture quotations are from the
King James Version of the Bible
Emphasis supplied unless otherwise indicated.

ISBN: 978-0-9821805-7-0

Published by FAST Missions
111 2nd Street
Kathryn, ND 58049

Additional copies of this book are available by
visiting us at WWW.FAST.ST

Revival Keys
Course Content

FAST *Revival Keys* is the third step of our three part training process designed to help you take in, live out, and then pass on the Word of God. It contains some of the most important information anywhere. In it, you are going to discover a step by step plan to pursue revival—the greatest and most urgent of all our needs!

The course consists of nine weeks of instruction. Each lesson includes small group training objectives, a Bible search, assigned memory verses, practical suggestions, supplemental resources, and more. Becoming a revival agent could mark a true turning point your life. Get ready!

1. Spiritual Ignition
2. Fire in My Bones
3. Candle of the Lord
4. Fanning the Flames
5. Detonation
6. Scattering Sparks
7. Combustion Engines
8. Walking Time Bombs
9. In Hot Pursuit

Please visit us online for supplemental resources including week by week teaching tips, promotional materials, quizzes, exams, certificates, memorization tools, and much more. You can also take this course in our online school: learn with students from around the world, ask questions, and interact with the author. For more information, please go to *WWW.FAST.ST/KEYS-GIFT*.

Spiritual Ignition

Week #1

Spiritual Ignition
Revival Keys > Week 1 > Memo

F

A

S

T

Memo:

When you look at what is happening in our world today, you can't help but sense things are spiraling out of control. That we are all sliding toward some imminent crisis. An intensity seems to be taking hold of people everywhere. And it all points to the soon return of Christ!

If that describes you, then you probably also feel a desire to climb higher in your walk with God. To give your life more fully to the cause of Christ. And to help others grow spiritually too. What you're really longing for is revival.

And that's what these *Revival Keys* lessons are all about. In the coming weeks, we are going to give you the skills and tools you need to become a revival agent. A revival among us is the greatest and most urgent of all our needs. And a big one is coming. Get ready!

**The Editor,
Hid in Christ**

Spiritual Ignition
Revival Keys > Week 1 > Objectives

Name: _____   Initialed by: _____

Date: _____

- ❏ Your first Bible Search is **II Kings 7:3-9**. This passage is a fascinating incident from the Old Testament that illustrates the blessings available to us through revival, blessings we tragically often miss out on. Ask for God's leading as you study, examine the passage carefully, and then fill in this week's study guide as best you can.

- ❏ Read the practical suggestions at the end of this booklet entitled **Conditions for Revival**. Be prepared to discuss them in detail at the next team meeting.

- ❏ Your first memory verse is **Ephesians 5:14**. If you have completed other FAST courses previously, take some extra time this week to review your other verses. If you are not familiar with the basic principles of Scripture memory, please take our free Crash Course on Bible memorization at *WWW.FAST.ST/CC*. You can do this!

- ❏ Review the supplemental resource entitled **The Agent Pledge**. If we are serious about wanting true revival, it is going to require personal commitment. Are you ready to go all in?

- ❏ Spend some special time this week praying God would impress each member of your team with a deeper sense of our need for revival. And that each would commit to seeking it earnestly in the weeks to come!

FAST
Finding A Savior Today

Spiritual Ignition
Revival Keys > Week 1 > Bible Search

Topic: II Kings 7:3-9

Brief Summary:

_____

_____

_____

_____

_____

_____

Observations/Insights:

_____

_____

_____

_____

_____

_____

_____

Principles & Applications:

1. _____

   _____

   _____

2. _____

   _____

   _____

3. _____

   _____

   _____

4. _____

   _____

   _____

Main Point:

_____

_____

_____

_____

Spiritual Ignition
Revival Keys > Week 1 > Practical Suggestions

Conditions for Revival
A revival among us is the greatest and most urgent of all our needs. To seek it should be our first work. Bible memorization can be a spark that quickens us spiritually. And a strong life of discipleship can be a powerful foundation for a spirit-filled life. But if we are ever to move on to becoming more effective in ministry, we are going to need something more. We will need the kind of power that comes in times of revival.

Revival will quicken our spiritual energies, our perceptions of duty, our commitment to Christ, and our faith in the purposes of God. It will illuminate our Bible study, and electrify our prayers. Revival awakens conviction for sin, true repentance, and a zeal to obey. And it gives us a heart for ministry, both within and without the church. In short, revival vitalizes every aspect of a person's Christian experience.

If you have never personally experienced an outpouring of the Holy Spirit, you are in for an exciting adventure in the weeks to come. We are going to explore exactly how to seek revival, spark it, and then safeguard the experience when it comes. Get ready!

The Four Essentials
Before getting too far into our study of revival, it is important to know a careful preparation is required. In particular, there are four conditions:

Diligent Study
The steps toward revival usually begin with a deeper experience in the Word. By getting more serious about internalizing Scripture. With learning how to identify biblical principles and turn them into practical projects. It comes as a result of learning to enter into real, intimate communication with the Master each morning.

As our skills in meditation and application develop, we learn to discern the voice of God's Spirit more clearly. The mysteries of the Bible begin to unlock. We stumble on to veins of truths never noticed or appreciated before. Like the two men on the road to Emmaus, our hearts begin to burn within us. This is the first step toward revival.

Earnest Prayer
Diligent study inspires the next step in the process of revival—earnest prayer. As the will of God becomes more clear, we begin to sense our need, and our unbelief. Motives and attitudes are revealed. Honest self-examination leads to a humbling of pride. Conviction awakens in the heart and we feel compelled to enter into the very presence of God, for pardon, and power to change.

We begin to learn how to wrestle with God, and take hold of divine strength through persevering faith. And the more we taste real victory, the more we long for even more of the Spirit. Repentance like this, is always an essential part of the preparation. Revival never comes, but in answer to prayer.

Committed Obedience
As our commitment to Christ deepens, our commitment to obedience will grow with it. We determine to get a better handle on our time. We seek a clearer sense of purpose, clearer priorities. We shift our schedule to give more room for God's will in our life. We get serious about tracking every task we need to do, and knocking them out faithfully. We strive to leave nothing undone.

We also start seeking out exhortation and accountability from others with similar desires. And we press together in pursuing the will of God. Our united heart cry becomes, "What would you have me to do?" And in time, God begins to reveal some plan.

Sacrificial Ministry
Usually that plan involves some kind of ministry. Some strategy to begin reaching out to others in our family, church, or community. The goodness of Christ, in blessing us so richly, compels us to find ways to bless others. We can't keep it to themselves. Our life fills with mission.

And we join with others in service, to attempt greater things than we could ever achieve by themselves. We're stretched beyond our comfort zone, and feel compelled to give sacrificially to the success of our project. At every challenge, we are driven to seek even more of God's presence and power. And God grants those requests. Ultimately, lives are won for the kingdom.

It's a simple, but tried and true recipe for revival: diligent study, earnest prayer, committed obedience, and sacrificial ministry. When the way is prepared, revival will come...

The Day of Pentecost

This is exactly what happened on the Day of Pentecost, isn't it? They had spent 10 days in the upper room, reviewing the words of Christ, the lessons He had taught them, the Scriptures He had explained to them. Gradually their understanding began to open. They became deeply convicted of their own shortcomings and failures, and began to seek God in humble confession, and repented of their unbelief. Through earnest prayer, their hearts were softened. And they resolved to do better. To live lives of faithfulness and integrity. They gave themselves more fully to the cause of Christ—His parting instructions to reach a lost world. The enormity of the task overwhelmed them, and they recognized only divine power could get the job done. They pled with God for the courage and boldness they needed. And when all was ready, those men and women in the upper room were electrified by the power of God.

It can happen again. And in fact, it has to. Revelation describes a time just before the return of Christ when John sees "another angel come down from heaven, having great power; and the earth was lightened with his glory" (Revelation 18:1). It's a hope filled promise. A time of great spiritual light and power. A time of awakening, of refreshing for God's people. A revival so vast it circles the globe.

Revelation is not the only place this revival is foretold. Habakkuk points to a time when the earth "filled with the knowledge of the glory of the LORD, as the waters cover the sea" (Habakkuk 2:14). Isaiah predicts a time when God will say to his people "arise, shine; for thy light is come, and the glory of the LORD is risen upon thee" (Isaiah 60:1). And then there's this promise in the book of Joel: "it shall come to pass afterward, that I will pour out my spirit upon all flesh" (Joel 2:28).

These, and many other verses, all describe one last great outpouring of the Holy Spirit. Earth's final revival. And it's just ahead for God's people! Which is why we must learn how to become a true revival agent...

Note: For more information about earth's final revival, and how internalizing Scripture can help us prepare for it, check out our book For Such a Time, by visiting us at WWW.FAST.ST.

Spiritual Ignition
Revival Keys > Week 1 > Illustration

The Agent Pledge

Revival is the greatest and most urgent of all our needs. To seek it should be our first work. But revival is not for the faint of heart!

While it can come in an instant, and when you least expect it, more likely, it will come after persevering in your pursuit of God for some time. Whether it is because He is testing our sincerity, some change needs to happen in our heart, or something else entirely—it's vital that we commit to seeking revival for the duration.

One of the best ways to stay focused on this goal is to write out a daily pledge and review it each morning briefly at the start of your devotions—to reset your commitment. If your purpose is to truly live as a revival agent, consider making our Agent Pledge, your pledge, each morning for the duration of this course. It's our vision of what it means to be a true revival agent:

> *I pledge to live today as an agent of revival for the Kingdom of God.*
>
> *An agent must commit to King Jesus daily, the promised Messiah, Savior, and Commander in Chief.*
>
> *An agent must receive daily instructions through direct communication with heaven, and carry out every assignment to the best of their ability.*
>
> *An agent must maximize their impact by continually improving every physical, mental, and spiritual power.*
>
> *An agent must commit to pursuing revival faithfully until the earth is lightened with the glory of God.*

Feel free to revise the wording as needed to make it truly yours. Then commit to renewing your pledge to God each morning—and see what God does!

Fire in My Bones

Week #2

Fire in My Bones
Revival Keys > Week 2 > Memo

F
A
S
T

Memo:

Hi again. Have you been thinking more about our need for revival? Better yet, have you committed to seeking it? I hope so. This week we are going to begin explore the conditions for revival more deeply. In particular, we are going to zoom in on the importance of serious Bible study in laying a foundation for revival.

If you have been a part of FAST for a while, you know the importance of Bible memorization as a way to jumpstart our Christian experience. And you know the importance of daily devotional study with an emphasis on personal application, to nourish and strengthen our walk with God. But to experience the kind of revival God wants for His people, we are going to have to dig deeper.

There are tremendous treasures hidden in the Word of God. And wrestling with these truths, personally, will go a long way towards preparing our hearts for revival. Give this week's study your best...

**The Editor,
Hid in Christ**

Fire in My Bones
Revival Keys > Week 2 > Objectives

Name: _____   Initialed by: _____

Date: _____

- ❏ Our Bible Search this week looks at **John 6:51-69**. In this passage, Jesus gives one of His clearest explanations about the place Scripture should have in our life. In fact, His words were so strong, many people turned their back on Him. Study the passage carefully—and note how you respond to what He said.

- ❏ Read the pages entitled **Searching the Word**, and use the suggestions to enrich your Bible Search this week. Bring any questions you have to your next team meeting. Knowing how to break down and apply key passages of Scripture is an important condition for revival.

- ❏ This week, your memory verse is **Psalms 119:18**. Come to the next team meeting prepared to quote this verse, along with last week's verse, word-perfect. And then keep reviewing these verses every day. Remember, our goal is not just to learn new verses, but also to not forget them!

- ❏ This week's supplemental resource covers five ways we can strengthen our intake of Scripture. Make sure each of these are a part of your life. It is entitled **Bible Internalization**.

- ❏ Continue praying this week that God would bring revival to you and your team. Ask specifically for God to give each of you rich insights to Scripture that would be like a fire in your bones.

FAST
Forsaking All Secular Thoughts

Fire in My Bones
Revival Keys > Week 2 > Bible Search

Topic: John 6:51-69

Brief Summary:

_____

_____

_____

_____

_____

_____

Observations/Insights:

_____

_____

_____

_____

_____

_____

Principles & Applications:

1. _____

2. _____

3. _____

4. _____

Main Point:

_____

Fire in My Bones
Revival Keys > Week 2 > Practical Suggestions

Searching the Word
The Bible is like no other book. Beyond the amazing details of its origin, preservation, and dissemination around the world, it claims for itself a unique status among all books: that of being inspired by God. "All Scripture is given by inspiration of God" (II Timothy 3:16). "Holy men of God spake as they were moved by the Holy Ghost" (II Peter 1:21). And the Spirit's presence can still be experienced in its pages today.

Jesus made this spiritual nature of the Bible clear: "the words that I speak unto you, they are spirit, and they are life" (John 6:63). And He promised those willing to study its pages, that the Spirit would "teach you all things", and "show you things to come" (John 14:26, 16:13). And ultimately, that the Spirit would reveal Christ in its pages (John 15:26). To those who ask, God offers to show "great and mighty things" (Jeremiah 33:3).

If you are serious about revival, you are going to have to tap deeper into the Bible's inexhaustible mysteries. And that means getting serious about study.

Study Methods
While there are many different approaches to Bible study, they generally fall into one of two categories: inductive or deductive. An inductive approach tends to focus on short challenging passages, drawing out principles—without imposing preconceived ideas on it. A deductive approach does the opposite. It starts with some concept or teaching, and then attempts to gather up and organize all the verses that support that view. Inductive study emphasizes application. Deductive study emphasizes proof.

While there is a valid place for both, an inductive approach is especially valuable to those seeking revival. Because it requires us to approach the Bible with an open heart, rather than preconceived ideas and beliefs, it clears a way for God to communicate with us individually. Because we are seeking to discern what a passage is saying, by examining the Bible directly, the Holy Spirit can show us things we have never noticed before. Grand themes that change how we look at life, self, the world, ministry and more. It is often these personal Spirit-led discoveries that sow the most powerful seeds for revival in our heart.

A Simple Plan

Thoughout our *Revival Keys* lessons, we will be encouraging you to take an inductive approach to studying one passage each week. We encourage you to take these studies seriously. Put your research skills to the stretch. Dig deep. Plead with God for insight. Allow the passage to speak for itself. And keep your focus on principles and personal application.

In the paragraphs below we'll outline a simple plan for inductive study. Follow these suggestions closely, and you may just make some discovery that will be like "a burning fire" shut up in your bones (Jeremiah 20:9).

1. *Prayer.* Before beginning, it is always important to invite the Holy Spirit to be our teacher and guide. Claim such promises as Jeremiah 33:3, James 1:5, and John 14:26. Second, take time to purpose in your heart that you will implement whatever it is you discover. See Ezra 7:10, James 1:22, etc. Relying on the Holy Spirit to teach you and committing yourself to acting on His revealed will are two vital conditions for receiving divine instruction. You are not really ready to begin, until you are determined to do whatever God says!

2. *Brief Summary.* Look up and familiarize yourself with the passage you will be studying. Read it through a couple times, paying careful attention to the words as you go. Look up any words you don't know in a dictionary. Review the larger context briefly. Read a different translation if it helps. Try to get a feel for what the writer is saying, and then paraphrase it briefly in your own words. Keep your notes short, and avoid going into analysis at this point. Simply summarize what the passage actually says.

3. *Observations/Insights.* Begin making notes about anything that strikes you as interesting. Are there any key words that seem especially important? What can you discover about them in a Greek or Hebrew lexicon, or a thesaurus? Use a concordance to find related verses—or if you have a study Bible, follow some of the cross references in it. Do any memorized verses come to mind? Take a few moments to gather some background information. Who wrote the passage? When? From where and to whom? What were the circumstances? Do you notice any patterns or some structure in the verses, or perhaps a recurring theme? Do not attempt to evaluate whether or not an insight is significant at this point. Just stay open-minded, and jot down anything interesting you discover as you explore.

4. *Principles & Applications.* Next, spend some time meditating on the passage. What are the three or four most important points the writer seems to be trying to get across? Is there a warning about some sin? Some advice or counsel? A character quality to imitate, or avoid? Some important warning, or command? Focus on those principles which seem most important to the passage and jot them down. Then, with each principles, take a moment to think through how you could apply it to your own life. What specific project could you do to build that truth into your life? Try to come up with some small plan of action for each key principle, and commit to following through.

5. *Main Point.* Finally, review the passage you have been studying once again, and all of your work so far. What seems to be the single most important theme of the passage? The central message? Wrestle with it until you can summarize what it is saying in a single brief sentence. You may need to revise that sentence a time or two to capture the essence of the passage more fully, or to make your wording more concise. Just keep at it—until you are satisfied with the result. Remember, one sentence only!

You Can Do It

It does not take any special abilities to become a Bible scholar—but it will take some effort. You don't have to go to seminary, or learn Greek and Hebrew. And you don't need a big library or expensive software tools. You don't even need exceptional intellect. A good study Bible, a decent concordance, and faith in God's Spirit to teach you is all you really need.

Of course, you can be sure the devil will do everything possible to hinder your efforts to get into the Word. He may whisper in your ear it's too hard, or that it's not your gift. Or he may simply try to keep you so busy you can't find time for deep study. Don't let it happen. Real revival takes real time in the Word.

Whisper the prayer of the Psalmist: "Open thou mine eyes, that I may behold wondrous things out of they law" (Psalms 119:18). Then crack open the Bible, begin your exploration in a spirit of anticipation—expecting God to speak, and quicken your heart (Psalms 119:93). What will God say?

Note: For more information about other approaches to Bible study, and how to build Scripture into your life, check out our Mighty in the Word study guides, by visiting us at WWW.FAST.ST.

Fire in My Bones
Revival Keys > Week 2 > Illustration

Bible Internalization

Want to maximize your internalization of Scripture? Build these five skills into your life, and you'll soon find your hold on God's Word growing stronger.

Listen to it taught: God has clearly gifted certain men and women with the ability to understand and explain the Scriptures effectively. Take advantage of those gifts! Listen regularly to good sermons, and take good notes. File the best information away, and you'll soon have an archive of valuable insights.

Read it for yourself: Reading through the Bible, gives you a broad overview that helps put the various parts of Scripture into context. It also helps you find those "special" verses which meet some need, but are hidden away in obscure locations. Read in any order and speed, but record each chapter you finish to ensure nothing gets missed. When it's all done, start over again.

Study it carefully: Systematic study of key words, doctrinal topics, Bible biographies, and special passages is needed to obtain a more accurate understanding of Scripture. Useful study tools include a concordance for looking up cross references, a Greek/Hebrew Lexicon to study the original meaning of words, and multiple translations, including a good interlinear. Other useful tools include a Bible dictionary, a thesaurus, and commentaries. Begin collecting these, and learn how to use them.

Memorize it often: Memorization enables you to keep the insights you gain through hearing, reading, and studying permanently fixed in your mind. It also helps keep the Scriptures accessible moment by moment. Set a pace for memorizing new verses every week, and stick to an effective review system.

Apply it to your life: The most important key to internalizing Scripture is implementation—building Scripture into our attitudes, choices, responses. Make sure you combine each method above with meditation and application. Whether you are listening to a sermon, reading some Old Testament book, doing an in-depth study of a passage, or memorizing some verse—application is what changes the life.

Candle of the Lord

Week #3

Candle of the Lord
Revival Keys > Week 3 > Memo

F
A
S
T

Memo:

Welcome back. This week, we look at another critical condition for revival. And what an important topic: persevering prayer. While there is nothing we need more than a greater outpouring of the Holy Spirit, it's often the thing we pray about least. How the angels of heaven must wonder sometimes!

Of course, there's a reason. Real prayer is the opening of our heart to God. Allowing Him to come in and show us our true condition, our true need. And that can be painful to do. Our human tendency is to avoid this kind of encounter at all costs.

But revival at its core is an encounter with God. It always shines light into the dark crevices of our character. Which just mean, revival only comes to those willing to face God in prayer...

**The Editor,
Hid in Christ**

Candle of the Lord
Revival Keys > Week 3 >Objectives

Name: _____   Initialed by: _____

Date: _____

- ❏ Our Bible Search this week looks at **I Kings 18:36-39**. It's a short passage—essentially a single prayer. But it led to one of the most powerful revivals in the Old Testament. Plus, I think you'll find it has some endtime implications as well. Dive in, and enjoy!

- ❏ This week's Practical Suggestions is entitled **In Answer to Prayer**. Read through this information prayerfully, asking God to help you assess your own prayer life accurately. Commit to making whatever changes God impresses on your heart.

- ❏ Your memory verse this week is probably less familiar than some of the others we have assigned, but it ties in well with the title of this lesson: **Proverbs 20:27**. Use this verse as a motivation to search your own heart as we continue our pursuit of revival.

- ❏ This week's supplemental resource gives **Keys to United Prayer**. Study it carefully, and come to your next team meeting prepared to give it a try. If you've never done this before, you are in for a treat.

- ❏ Since our focus this week is on prayer, let's step things up a bit. If you haven't yet done so, add a prayer request to your prayer journal, specifically for revival. Better still, move it to the very front of the stack. And make a commitment to pray over it every day!

FAST
Fervently Asking for Spiritual Treasures

Candle of the Lord
Revival Keys > Week 3 > Bible Search

Topic: I Kings 18:36-39

Brief Summary:

_____

_____

_____

_____

_____

_____

Observations/Insights:

_____

_____

_____

_____

_____

_____

Principles & Applications:

1. _____

   _____

   _____

2. _____

   _____

   _____

3. _____

   _____

   _____

4. _____

   _____

   _____

Main Point:

_____

_____

_____

_____

Candle of the Lord
Revival Keys > Week 3 > Practical Suggestions

In Answer to Prayer

Revival only comes in answer to prayer. That is because prayer alone can prepare us for revival. Bible study can show us our true condition, but only through prayer can we bring our heart to the one who can heal us. So if you are serious about revival, you must press deeper into the mysteries of prayer.

Of course, growing in prayer is not easy. Many long for a more intimate prayer life, but they are not quite sure how to pursue it. The paragraphs ahead can help, by giving you important insights into how you can fill your prayer time with more of the Spirit's presence. Follow these tips carefully, and they will make prayer a more earnest, and fervent part of your life.

Getting Organized

Organizing your requests into a prayer journal is a great first step in strengthening your prayer life. We recommend using a loose leaf notebook and storing each request on a separate sheet of paper. Each sheet should include a request, a specific verse or two, and a log of the dates you pray over it, along with details on how God is working. We recommend separating your request into one section for daily, priority requests, and another for regular requests you pray through less often. If you've taken our *Basic Training* course, you know a prayer journal can be effective at reminding you to pray for things you would otherwise forget.

But a prayer journal can strengthen your prayer life in other ways, if you use it correctly. Here are three things to assess in your prayer journal use:

- Is there a good mix of requests in your prayer journal? If you are only praying for personal needs, and a few friends or relatives going through challenges, you may be thinking too small. Put in a request to grow in some character quality. Or for greater victory over some temptation that haunts you. Pray for important goals, projects at work, or guidance on big decisions. Pray for evangelism in some specific country, or for some ministry you respect. Add names of specific people you would like to see come to Christ. Or who are struggling spiritually. And of course, put in a prayer for revival. The more you connect prayer to every part of your life the more meaningful it will become.

- Look at your notes. Are you only jotting down the dates each time you pray? Or are you also jotting down insights as you pray connected with each request? Prayer is as much about hearing as it is about talking. So try to learn to listen for the voice of God when praying. Is God working in some way? Jot it down. Is there some step God would have you take? Jot it down. Has God given you some insight into the reasons for that situation? Or what His will might be? Jot it down. Prayer becomes more powerful when it transforms into two-way communication. And often, it is that communication which leads to answers.

- Review the verses used in your requests. Was your request triggered by some verse you stumbled onto in your personal Bible study? Or did you come up with a request, and then seek out a verse that seemed to fit? Or to put it differently, are you telling God what to do? Or is God telling you what to pray? Learning to look for God to show us His purposes, and then trying to focus our requests on those purposes, can revolutionize our prayer life and transform it into an exciting journey. In short, try to include more requests inspired by Scripture.

While a prayer journal is a powerful tool, its real benefit comes from teaching you how to connect prayer to every part of your life, how to discern God working in response to your requests, and how to link your prayers more closely with Scripture. This kind of prayer is key to revival.

Scriptural Praying

As we grow in our walk with God, the connection between Scripture and prayer tends to become more and more evident. We see how deep Bible study requires a deep attitude of prayer. And similarly, we experience how God speaks back through Scripture, when we present our requests. Ultimately, the link between prayer and Scripture grows so close, it becomes difficult to distinguish between them.

Which suggests the value of using Scripture itself as a framework for prayer. How? Here's what we recommend. First, find a passage appropriate to your situation and turn to it in your Bible. Then, simply go through that passage verse by verse, taking a moment or two to talk with God about what each verse says, personalizing it, and adapting it to your specific need. And then listen for God to speak back through that verse. After a few moments, proceed to the next verse. Go as fast or as slow as you want.

If you want to focus on building character, turn to the beatitudes and ask God to build each of those qualities into your life. Or you could pray through the Ten Commandments, and ask God to search your heart for pockets of sin you may not be aware of. Or you could pray through Ephesians 6, and ask God to arm you with each piece of spiritual armor listed there. And that is just the beginning.

Many Psalms are perfect for seasons of praise. Others for times of confession, and other for times of crisis. Try praying through a string of proverbs—asking God for divine wisdom. Paul's epistles are filled with amazing prayers for God's will to be done in the lives of those he was writing. Pray these for yourself, or use them to intercede for a friend. And there are many prayers recorded in Scripture by Bible writers that can serve as models for other needs. Even parables and familiar Bible stories, can sometimes be adapted to situations in your life. The more you look, the more you will find.

Setting aside special times for this kind of prayer will take your prayer to a whole new level. It changes prayer into a divine encounter within the Word.

Prayer for Revival

A prayer journal is a great way to organize your requests, and it can teach you important lessons about prayer. Scriptural praying is a powerful way to seek God on specific topics using the Bible itself. But the highest form of prayer may well be prayer for revival itself.

If we are serious about seeking revival, it begins with our own heart. Pleading with God for the power of the Holy Spirit, requires us to be transparent before God. Allowing Him to shine light into the deepest corners of our heart. To show us our hidden thoughts and intents. The motives that drive us. If you want an outpouring of God's Spirit, you must learn to wrestle with God. And that takes time.

Make this wrestling a priority each day. Ask God to give you that fully surrendered heart. And don't stop praying until revival comes...

Note: For more information about different approaches to prayer, and to explore some of the Bible's greatest prayers, check out our Power in Prayer study guides, by visiting us at WWW.FAST.ST.

Candle of the Lord
Revival Keys > Week 3 > Illustration

Keys to United Prayer

Praying alone is important, but praying with others brings its own blessings. Jesus gave promises specifically related to united prayer (Matthew 18:19-20), and the book of Acts clearly shows its power (Acts 1:14, 2:1, 4:31). One of the best ways to encourage strong united prayer is to pray conversationally. (Sometimes this is called popcorn prayer, or sentence prayers). Here's a brief description of how it works:

- Appoint a leader to begin and end the prayer. This person can also transition the group through each section of the prayer.
- Follow an organized progression. We suggest the acronym WAIT: start with a time of *worship*, move to *admitting* our need, then *intercession*, and finally *thanksgiving*. The leader announces each transition.
- Each person prays as they are prompted by the Holy Spirit. They do not need to pray in any order, and can pray as often as they wish.
- Keep each prayer brief—only a sentence or two at a time. Pray about one thing, then give others a chance to pray. Some may wish to affirm another person's request. Avoid long individual prayers.
- Don't use formal phrases to begin and end each individual prayer—such as "Father in heaven" or "In Jesus's name." It is all one prayer, prayed together as a group.
- Feel free to quote a verse of Scripture or a line from a familiar hymn if the Holy Spirit impresses you to do so.
- Don't feel uncomfortable with periods of silence. As this type of prayer becomes more natural, timid members will start to join in and there will be less silence. Rather, use the quietness to ask God what He would have YOU pray for.
- When it is time to stop, the appointed person should present the entire prayer to God in the name of Jesus—thus making it clear the prayer session has come to a end.

Give the method a try, and you will soon discover that approaching prayer like this in a group can knit your hearts together in powerful ways.

Fanning the Flames

Week #4

Fanning the Flames
Revival Keys > Week 4 > Memo

F
A
S
T

Memo:

Ready for another challenging study? I hope so, because this week we are going to talk about how to fan the flames of revival.

Have you ever seen someone try to start a campfire? They gather all the kindling into a pile, and strike a match. The flame starts out tiny, and vulnerable. But if you blow on it gently, it burns hotter and starts to spread. Pretty soon you are throwing on logs, and the fire is raging. That's what we are talking about today...

The Bible studies we've been doing are those little pieces of kindling. And prayer is what strikes the match. This week we are going to look at how exhortation fans the flame. Are you ready?

The Editor,
Hid in Christ

Fanning the Flames
Revival Keys > Week 4 > Objectives

Name: _____   Initialed by: _____

Date: _____

- ❏ This week's Bible Search is **Acts 11:19-26**. It focuses in on one of my favorite Bible characters, whose ministry helped build one of the most powerful training centers of the New Testament. A revival, actually. Take some time to dig deep into the passage and try to discern the secret to his success.

- ❏ Read the material ahead entitled **Encouraging Exhortation**. As you do, reflect on your participation in your team. Are you encouraging, challenging, and supporting others to achieve their very best? Are you modeling that, by giving your best?

- ❏ This week's memory verse is **Hebrews 3:13-14**. It describes the dangers of neglecting biblical fellowship, and the promised blessing that comes with it. Be ready to quote this at your next team meeting, along with all your other verses so far. Remember, always review reference-verse-reference.

- ❏ If we are serious about revival, we are going to have to get serious about putting away known sin. This week's supplemental resource offers a simple strategy for **Victory over Sin**. And it works...

- ❏ Keep up your prayer focus on revival. This week, try to make a point of praying for each member of your team by name. Ask God to work mightily in each one, giving them a greater desire for obedience. And a greater determination to pursue revival.

FAST
Focused on Accomplishing Specific Tasks

Fanning the Flames
Revival Keys > Week 4 > Bible Search

Topic: Acts 11:19-26

Brief Summary:

_____

_____

_____

_____

_____

_____

Observations/Insights:

_____

_____

_____

_____

_____

_____

Principles & Applications:

1. _____

   _____

   _____

2. _____

   _____

   _____

3. _____

   _____

   _____

4. _____

   _____

   _____

Main Point:

_____

_____

_____

_____

Fanning the Flames
Revival Keys > Week 4 > Practical Suggestions

Encouraging Exhortation
Powerful revivals are always rooted in real discipleship. But real discipleship takes commitment. Staying faithful in prayer, Bible study, or Scripture memory is hard. Consistent obedience can be a struggle. Trying to witness is tough. But the Bible gives us a remedy: "exhort one another daily ... lest any of you be hardened through the deceitfulness of sin" (Hebrews 3:13). We need exhortation. The challenge and encouragement of fellow Christians to help us press on. And that is important, for we are only "made partakers of Christ" if we stay "stedfast unto the end" (Hebrews 3:14).

The best place to get this kind of exhortation is in a small team of committed believers. A group where each member shares the same goal of deeper discipleship. A group where each person is willing to support and encourage one another. A group serious about living for Christ. A group determined to pursue revival. In the paragraphs ahead, we'll share a few keys to building this kind of group.

Emphasize Obedience
The first step in encouraging exhortation is to inspire each group member to see the importance of personal obedience to God. Obedience is not only key to inheriting eternal life (Revelation 22:14), it is also key to nearly every other area of discipleship. It is key to understanding the Word of God (John 7:17). Key to power in prayer (Psalms 66:18). And key to effective witnessing, too (I Thessalonians 1:5). And you can't get around the importance of obedience in terms of revival. The Bible makes it clear: God only gives "the Holy Ghost ... to them that obey him" (Acts 5:32).

Practically, this often plays out in the accountability period of your team meetings. Are you serious about checking over each person's objectives to make sure they are done? Or is this part of the meeting minimized. Is there a real expectation assignments will be completed? Or are there embarassed chuckles about skipping a few items? If some task proves difficult, is there a problem solving mindset—determined to identify the obstacle and find some way to break through it? Does one member's difficulty become the burden of the entire group, or is everyone left to sink or swim on their own?

These are not easy questions. And granted, not everyone will want this kind of engagement. But the reality is, most Christians will never rise to their full potential, without a clear challenge, strong support, and genuine accountability. Put simply, exhortation is essential. And those who long for revival will be drawn to a team like this.

Alertness to Application

In addition to cultivating a strong accountability period in your team, it's also important for your team to develop a mindset of application. After many years, working with countless groups, I've become convinced personal application is the one thing human nature most seeks to avoid. Yet it's essential for real transformation. If your team truly wants to grow, each member of your team must determine to overcome this tendency.

Application is powered by a simple commitment to act on God's Word, and implement it personally. It's a determination to be a "doer of the word", and not just a hearer only (James 1:22). And while the best place to practice application is in the quiet and privacy of our own personal devotions, you can definitely encourage application in a team.

Perhaps a friend will share something that spoke to them during their Bible study, in a memory verse, or through something in these practical suggestions. Or they may simply express a longing to grow in some area, or to achieve some goal. Such "good intentions" can pop up at any time—so be alert!

You can help a person transform "potential" applications like these, into a concrete plan of action by asking simple questions. Surround yourself with people who are skilled in asking such questions and learn to ask them yourself:

- Are you serious about doing that?
- What would that look like, in practical terms?
- What is keeping you from doing that?
- What steps of action would that require?
- What can you do this week to get started?
- Anyone have insights into how to make this happen?
- Is there some way I can help you with that?
- Is this something our team could work on together?
- Are we really willing to commit to this?

If some friend commits to a plan of action: make a note, and add it to your prayer journal so you can pray for them. And then follow up. Ask how it went the next time you meet. Exhortation helps hold our feet to the fire by catching us when we're talking in generalities, calling us to specific steps of action, and then encouraging us along the way. It is how Christians grow into the fullness of Christ (Ephesians 4:15).

Accountability only works when there is a shared strong motivation. A desire to get real in our walk with God, together. A longing to help one another become all we can be. Ask God to awaken that kind of motivation in the heart of every person on your team.

Biblical Exhortation

Exhortation is biblical. And as believers, we must see the importance of challenging one another if we are ever to reach our full potential in Christ. In the New Testament we see a clear pattern of exhortation. Barnabas, when he went to Antioch, "exhorted them all, that with purpose of heart they would cleave unto the Lord. For he was a good man, and full of the Holy Ghost" (Acts 11:23). Likewise, He and Paul "exhorted" the new disciples in Lystra and Iconium, "to continue in the faith" (Acts 14:22). And later Paul, traveling all over Macedonia, gave them "much exhortation" (Acts 20:2). To the believers at Thessalonica, Paul wrote: we "exhort you by the Lord Jesus" that ye would "abound more and more" (I Thessalonians 4:1).

Sadly, few Christians appreciate the importance of exhortation today. We love to study, talk about, or even argue over Scripture—but we struggle to bring the Word of God to bear on our own personal lives. And we're not very good at encouraging others to practically apply Scripture either. As a result, there is widespread spiritual immaturity.

To correct this, we must rediscover the gentle art of exhortation, and band together with fellow believers who are serious about strengthening their walk with God. Make yourself part of a team like this, and you are sure to find your self growing spiritually. And it may just lead to revival.

Note: For more information about how to grow in personal obedience, and be more Spirit led, check out our Down to Business study guides, by visiting us at WWW.FAST.ST.

Fanning the Flames
Revival Keys > Week 4 > Illustration

Victory Over Sin

The Bible teaches clearly there is power for victory in the Gospel. But when it comes to the nitty, gritty, we don't always know how to obtain it. One key is simply understanding that the Gospel which saves us initially, is what empowers us moment by moment. "As ye have therefore received Christ Jesus the Lord, so walk ye in him" (Colossians 2:6). In other words, the ABC's of the Bible through which we receive Christ, are what give victory in the moment of temptation. Consider these points:

> *Admit:* Admit our inability to do right. Acknowledge the problem of sin. That it is embedded in our nature. That we are in a desperate condition. That without help, we are powerless.
>
> *Believe:* Believe Christ paid the penalty we deserve. And as a result, we can have full forgiveness and pardon for sin. That Christ's blood moves us into a new relationship with God, with full access to His grace.
>
> *Claim:* Claim the power of the Holy Spirit. Everything we need for right living is within our reach, right now. The available power is limitless. We just need to take hold of it by faith.

So what do you do when tempted by some desire to do wrong? Turn to the Gospel. Flash a prayer to heaven along these lines. First ADMIT: "Lord, you know I'm drawn to this. I'm weak. I can't resist this alone." Then BELIEVE: "Thank you for Jesus, who died on the cross. I plead His blood—receive me." And last CLAIM: "Please, give me the strength to overcome. Grant me your power, right now." Then in faith, turn away.

Sometimes the victory is easy. The temptation is broken and we're free. But other times, we waiver, and look back. What do we do then? Fire off another prayer: "Lord, I can't do this without help. I plead the blood of Christ. And I take hold of your power, now." Then turn away again. Depending on the strength of the temptation, it may take several rounds more. But so long as you cling to the gospel, you cannot be overcome. The gospel never fails.

Detonation

Week #5

Detonation
Revival Keys > Week 5 > Memo

F

A

S

T

Memo:

Welcome back to Revival Keys. We hope you are starting to sense the first hints of revival, as we've pressed deeper into the calling and privileges of every Christian. The promise is sure: when the way is prepared, revival will come.

There's one last condition for revival we need to look at today: ministry. Revival will only go just so far—if you try to keep it to yourself. The Spirit of God is always seeking to burst out in ministry to the people around us. It can't be bottled up or contained. If we want more of His power, we must open the doors for God to reach out through us.

If you are ready to launch out into the deep, you will soon be equipped to serve as a true revival agent.

**The Editor,
Hid in Christ**

Detonation
Revival Keys > Week 5 > Objectives

Name: _____   Initialed by: _____

Date: _____

- ☐ Complete a Bible Search on **Luke 5:1-11**. This passage is a story from the life of Jesus that is filled with amazing lessons for ministry. Take some time to dig deep, and draw out its most important principles. Then come to your next meeting ready to share your discoveries!

- ☐ Read the section entitled **A Heart for Ministry**. As you do, commune with God about the points presented. Ask God to spark ideas about how you might be able to implement them. Which possibilities appeal most to you? Come prepared to discuss what you learn about yourself with the others on your team.

- ☐ Memorize **John 4:35**. This is one of my favorite verses about ministry. Among other things, it highlights the best time to begin. Are you ready to try something big?

- ☐ This week's supplemental resource gives a **Ministry Checklist** you can use to build an unleashed ministry. Look for ways to strengthen any existing ministries you are involved with, or use it to sketch out an all new plan to reach your community.

- ☐ Are you still praying each day for revival, and for the members of your team specifically? This week, continue asking God to work on each heart, that each would sense a clear call from heaven to give their lives more fully to service.

FAST
Freely Announcing Salvation Together

Detonation

Revival Keys > Week 5 > Bible Search

Topic: Luke 5:1-11

Brief Summary:

_____

_____

_____

_____

_____

_____

Observations/Insights:

_____

_____

_____

_____

_____

_____

_____

Principles & Applications:

1. _____

_____

_____

2. _____

_____

_____

3. _____

_____

_____

4. _____

_____

_____

Main Point:

_____

_____

_____

_____

Detonation
Revival Keys > Week 5 > Practical Suggestions

A Heart for Ministry

Before returning to heaven, Jesus left the church a clear assignment—to reach a lost world with the good news of salvation. And for 2000 years, the church has been pursuing that goal. It still stands today as our mission. The reason the church exists.

But in many churches, there seems to be little real soul-winning power. We're busy with the endless array of activities needed to keep our programs going, but few come to Christ. And the impact in our community is negligible. What's needed is power. The power that comes from revival.

But ministry is also a condition for revival. God wants to give power for service, but He is looking for individuals committed to imparting the blessings they receive to others. Who desire to be channels of grace. When God sees workers determined to reach their communities in service, He knows they are safe to entrust with blessings. And He will grant them the blessing they seek.

In other words, if your team is serious about revival, it needs to get serious about getting plugged in to ministry.

Personal Engagement

The first step in activating your team is for each member to give some serious thought to developing a personal evangelistic strategy, and then commit to working at it weekly. Listed below are some simple ministries, team members could try, just to stimulate your creativity. Feel free to come up with your own wildly creative and radical ideas.

- Mail out fliers to addresses in a specific neighborhood, offering some free book. Deliver the books personally and invite them to a small group in the area meeting weekly to discuss the book.
- Operate a small correspondence school. Advertise it on social media, and send out lessons each week by mail to whoever enrolls.
- Conduct telephone surveys—offering those that complete your survey a free DVD on some interesting topic. Follow up with each person later, to make sure they received it, and to see if they would like more information.

- Use local newspaper ads to promote a video lending library, and send out one DVD at a time to those who respond until they have watched a whole series.
- Host a small dinner club in your home, for a few friends, featuring some vegetarian recipe and a short video on Bible secrets to health.
- Announce a free class at your local library on Bible memorization and lead those that respond through a short course like the *Survival Kit*.
- Pick a neighborhood and drop off a series of tracts or pamphlets, one each week, at every door. At the end of the series, drop off a survey and invite them to mail back their response to the information.

This list is hardly exhaustive—the possibilities are endless. And you can mix and match aspects of these in different ways. To be most effective though, a good plan needs to incorporate three core aspects of witnessing: contacting those who are spiritually hungry, connecting with them relationally, and ultimately, communicating Bible truth. Try to incorporate all three into your plan. And keep tweaking your plan, until your ministry begins to see results.

Working Together

As important as personal engagement is, ministry is most effective when different people work together. This was the plan Jesus followed with his disciples (See Mark 3:14), and Paul followed it in his missionary journeys as well (See Acts 20:4). We need the encouragement and support only a team can provide. A group also has access to a greater pool of knowledge, abilities, and resources. And working together means each person can function in the role that best matches their gifts and abilities.

When God puts a team together, it is like a body—with all the organs and parts necessary for ministry. Consider a scenario like the following: One member, who enjoys going door to door, finds interests he then enrolls in another member's correspondence school. Later as they learn more, they are encouraged to join a small group that meets in still another member's home. And at some point, another team member may offer personal studies to further deepen their Bible knowledge. The team is there at every stage, working together to assist those individuals in their spiritual journey. In working together, your team has everything you need to win souls!

But how to you go from a bunch of separate, individual ministries, into a single shared team ministry? It involves two basic steps:

First, your team needs to agree to focus in on some specific group in your community: Homeschool families. Young professionals. Couples wanting to strengthen their marriage. Students at a local college. People interested in health, or endtime events, or parenting. Even a specific neighborhood or section of town. These groups are everywhere, we just need to learn to start seeing the invisible. Focusing on one target enables you to fine tune and optimize each aspect of our ministry to reach that group—dramatically enhancing your effectiveness. So start by settling on some specific group.

Second, identify the steps people in that exact group will have to pass through to reach faith in Christ. Think of these steps as planks in a long rope bridge crossing some chasm. Even one or two missing planks is all it takes to stop people from making it across. How will you advertise to them? What offer will most appeal to them? How can connect with them personally, and grow those relationships? What resources will best introduce them to Scripture? And maintain their interest? You may not have answers to all these questions now, but if you start moving forward, you'll learn more as you go.

Your team meetings then, involve ensuring each step in that pathway is supported by some member of your team. And that the entire process is working well. Your team guides seekers through every transition together.

Aim for Excellence

You won't know how good that plan is, until you put it to the test. You may experience immediate success—or seeming failure. Either way, commit to pressing forward. Carefully evaluate each step in your ministry strategy and tweak any steps that do not work as well you would like. Keep learning and improving as you go. Over time, your plan will likely end up far different from what you originally envisioned. Just keep pursuing success.

When God sees a true heart for ministry, He knows you are safe to entrust with spiritual power, for you will use it to bless others. Sacrificial ministry, combined with diligent study, earnest prayer, and committed obedience is the final condition for revival.

Note: For more information about building a ministry that reaches your community more effectively, check out our Unleashed study guides, by visiting us at WWW.FAST.ST.

Detonation
Revival Keys > Week 5 > Illustration

Ministry Checklist

Ministries are like bridges that bring people from first contact to faith in Christ. Here are seven planks we recommend building into every ministry bridge:

The Valentine: How are you going to tell people about the problem you help solve? A flier? Poster? Newspaper ad? Facebook post? Etc. Think of these as valentines, saying I like you, do you like me?

The Mousetrap: Your valentine needs to include a bit of bait. An offer of some free gift in return for their contact information. By showing interest in your solution, they open the door to a new relationship.

The Fishbowl: Next, use that contact info to establish consistent, ongoing communication. Usually this is a newsletter of some sort with free content each week. This helps them get to know you, and builds your credibility.

The Ladder: Two or three times a year, promote some program related to their area of interest. Usually these will be done online or by mail. Use your newsletter to promote it and see who signs up. Design the interaction so it deepens the relationship.

The Microphone: Invite those who do your program to a small live event. It can be a graduation, a banquet, a concert, speaker or something else. This is your chance to meet them in person. Make a good impression!

The Loveseat: Organize your event with the specific purpose of encouraging attendees to join a small group. Make the transition as seamless as possible, by making them a natural follow up to your meeting. Small groups cultivate strong relationships.

The Teapot: Finally, invite these new friends to your next evangelistic meeting. Your relationship is what brings them, and keeps them coming.

Scattering Sparks

Week #6

Scattering Sparks
Revival Keys > Week 6 > Memo

F

A

S

T

Memo:

The Editor here, and I'm excited to announce we've reached an important milestone. We've finally covered all the essential conditions for revival. Which means it's time at last to zoom in on an actual strategy for revival.

Revival is the solution to a problem plaguing churches everywhere. The lack of spiritual vitality. Spiritual commitment. Spiritual engagement. It's everywhere, isn't it?

Somehow the enemy has shackled up thousands of believers, keeping them from the Spirit-filled life. This week we look at how to start breaking those chains. While the problem is serious, the solution is simple. At least, to a revival agent...

**The Editor,
Hid in Christ**

Scattering Sparks
Revival Keys > Week 6 > Objectives

Name: _____   Initialed by: _____

Date: _____

- ❏ This week's Bible Search is on **Ezekiel 37:1-10**. And it is one of the most dramatic visions anywhere in the Bible. It depicts a dreadful situation, but also gives plenty of hope. And there's no doubt this passage is talking about revival. Get ready for a great study!

- ❏ Read the section entitled **A Strategy for Revival** and give it prayerful thought. Just think—God might use you to bring revival to your church. It could happen! Just ask God how you can be part of the solution, and then come prepared to share what He puts on your heart.

- ❏ Begin memorizing **Luke 11:13**. If you haven't already added this verse to the request in your prayer journal for revival, do it now. These is also a great verse to claim for whatever revival plan your team pulls together. Be sure to learn it word-perfect!

- ❏ This week's supplemental resource is a **Revival Meeting Checklist**. Use it to begin sketching out a basic plan for revival in your church. Are you ready for this?

- ❏ The real purpose of these lessons is not just revival for you, or even revival for your team. It's to see revival come to your entire church. Plead this week for revival to break out all through your congregation. And keep praying for it, till it comes!

FAST
Final Army's Scripture Training

Scattering Sparks
Revival Keys > Week 6 > Bible Search

Topic: Ezekiel 37:1-10

Brief Summary:

___

___

___

___

___

___

Observations/Insights:

___

___

___

___

___

___

Principles & Applications:

1. _____
   _____
   _____

2. _____
   _____
   _____

3. _____
   _____
   _____

4. _____
   _____
   _____

Main Point:

_____
_____
_____
_____

Scattering Sparks
Revival Keys > Week 6 > Practical Suggestions

A Strategy for Revival

As we've mentioned before, our greatest and most urgent need is revival. Earth's final scenes are stacking up all around us, like a long chain of dominoes. And we know when things finally begin to happen, those dominoes will topple in quick succession. The final movements will be rapid ones!

And yet at the same time, there seems to be a lack of spiritual vitality in many congregations. Most churches have plateaued or are in decline. Few do any real discipleship training. And the outreach programs you do find, are typically cookie cutter imitations of each other, that have long since lost any real soul winning effectiveness.

Somehow the enemy has lulled us into ministry complacency. When we should be more awake and energetic than ever, we seem to be dozing at our post. Our only hope of beoming engaged and effective once again, is revival. But to pursue it we need a clear strategy. The paragraphs ahead give the steps we recommend taking.

Kindle the Core

Revival must start with you—and your team. It is usually in the intense fellowship of a small group bound by real commitment that revival first ignites. Rarely does revival blaze hot or burn long in an isolated individual.

It wasn't until the disciples finally pulled together at Pentecost that revival broke out in the early church. Similarly, your team must pull together. There must be aggressive memorization of the Word. Diligent study and earnest prayer. A serious commitment to personal obedience. And a genuine heart for ministry. All the things we have talked about so far. The essential conditions for revival. Once these are in place, your team will be ready to get serious about seeking Revival.

The genesis of a churchwide revival could be just around the corner, but it will start first by burning brightly in the midst of some team. A team determined to seek revival. A team determined to let nothing stand in the way. That team could be yours!

Invest in People

Next, start reaching out, outside your team. How? By taking an interest in the spiritual lives of other church members. There are sincere Christians everywhere longing to grow in Bible study, prayer, personal obedience, and in ministry. And you have the tools to help them. We all, at times, need the encouragement and challenge of a fellow Christian—and you can be that friend for someone else. Make it your team motto: each one, reach one.

The best way to find interested people, is to start sharing fresh, personal testimonies about how God is working in your life, and notice who seems drawn to what you share. Keep an eye out for Christians with a desire to grow in their walk with God. Maybe they are interested in memorizing Scripture. Maybe they want to develop a more consistent devotional life. Maybe they want a prayer partner to pray with over some urgent need. Maybe they are struggling with some besetting sin and need support. Or maybe they just want to get involved in outreach or ministry. Offer to help wherever their motivation seems strongest!

Granted, this can be costly in terms of time, but there's no other way to help people grow. And there is nothing better to deepen your own walk with God, than to help someone else. And ultimately, it will be through these relationships that revival spreads: life to life.

Public Meetings

Once your team is regularly pleading for an outpouring of the Holy Spirit in your church, and the members are busy investing in the lives of people in your church, it will be time to start thinking about public meetings. Consider a week-end series, or a special week of prayer, or even a special sermon. Plan it well, leaving no detail to.

Bring in an appropriate speaker, enlist the pastor, or choose someone from your own team. Arrange uplifting music, and schedule in some riveting testimonies. Choose topics that exalt the Word of God, our need to lay it up, live it out, and pass it on. Emphasize the shortness of time and our urgent need for revival. Conclude with a solemn appeal to deeper commitment.

Public meetings like this, are God's ordained means of revival. And God longs to bless your church. When that way is prepared, revival will come.

Safeguard the Experience

Don't be surprised when real revival breaks out. Rather, anticipate it. The whole church, of course, will never be fully revived—but without fail, the hearts of some will always be touched. And often, the people you least expect! I'm not talking about the presence of the Spirit we sense on a day to day basis, but real demonstrations of power. Heartfelt conviction. Tears. Sincere repentance. Earnest testimonies. I've seen many revivals of this sort in my life. And I've known countless others who have described similar experiences. Revival may be rare, but it is very real.

It's important to have a plan in place, should revival break out, to give those who respond to your meetings an opportunity to deepen and preserve their experience. And the best way to do that is to get them into a training team as quickly as possible. If you have been part of FAST for some time, you know the progression we recommend:

1. Begin with the *Survival Kit*, and nail down the basics of Bible memorization. The internalization of Scripture is the spark that quickens the heart.
2. Move on to *Basic Training*, and the basic skills of discipleship. Bible study, prayer, time management and personal witnessing are the foundation for lasting revival.
3. And finally, lead them through *Revival Keys* and urge them to become a revival agents. Ultimately, the only way to maintain revival, is to work at sharing it with others.

Don't underestimate the importance of this follow-up. God is unlikely to bring revival to more people than you are ready to care for. But when that preparation is ready to go, revival can go from being a mere weekend event to a lasting turning point in someone's life. With systematic training in place, the flame will just burn brighter and brighter, until they too are filled with a sense of urgency and purpose. Rather than fizzling out, revival can become a raging fire that spreads through your entire church.

Note: For more information about God's plan for the church, and how to engage in it more fully, check out our Jump Start study guides, by visiting us at WWW.FAST.ST.

Scattering Sparks
Revival Keys > Week 6 > Illustration

Revival Meeting Checklist

Revival cannot be forced. It is God's sovereign will that decides when and where He will send it. But the conditions for revival can be met. And special events can be scheduled to create opportunities for God to manifest His power. These can be a weekend retreat, a week of prayer, or even a single sermon. Here's a short checklist of things to keep in mind when planning your next revival meeting.

- Plan the meetings together as a team. God loves to bless the efforts of a group working together with a shared vision and purpose.
- Spend serious time in prayer, both before and during the meetings.
- Get approval from the appropriate leaders in your church. Schedule it some time in advance, and try to avoid any major conflicts in the church calendar.
- Choose a speaker. If you bring in an outside speaker, make sure he understands your goals. Or your pastor may wish to lead out. Sometimes, the most effective messages will be simple talks given by members of your team.
- Build anticipation. Have the members of your team share their hopes and dreams for the meetings with friends in the days leading up to the event. Generate anticipation.
- Involve others in the church. Ask people to help with the sound equipment, lead song service, do a children's program, or special music. Getting people to help, will get them to come.
- Promote the meetings heavily through bulletin inserts, verbal announcements, posters in the foyer, and personal invitations.
- Personal testimonies can be powerful. Have members of your team share what God is doing in their life—as part of every presentation.
- Be sure to conclude your meetings with a strong appeal. Invite them to come forward for a prayer of commitment.
- Have a training team ready to launch shortly after the meetings. Keep sign up sheets available, and urge people to join in.
- Don't forget to report back to the church about the positive results of the meetings. And then start thinking about your next event!

Combustion Engines

Week #7

Combustion Engines
Revival Keys > Week 7 > Memo

F

A

S

T

Memo:

These last three weeks, we are going to look at some of the most exciting lessons in the entire course. And this week's topic is a big one: You are about to learn how to build a combustion engine.

A combustion engine is actually pretty amazing. You put a small amount of fuel inside a block of metal and ignite it. The explosive power of that fire, when captured within a motor and directed toward a useful purpose can accomplish extraordinary things. In fact, our whole modern industrial world, can largely be traced back to James Watt figuring out how to make a steam engine. Without it, we'd probably still be riding horses.

The same thing can happen in our teams. By organizing ourselves into combustion engines, we have the potential to unleash incredible power. Ready to learn how? Keep reading...

**The Editor,
Hid in Christ**

Combustion Engines
Revival Keys > Week 7 > Objectives

Name: _____   Initialed by: _____

Date: _____

- ❏ For this week's Bible search, our focus is **Deuteronomy 20:1-9**. It's a fascinating passage about what to do before going out to war. Seeking revival is war, against an invisible and powerful enemy. Which makes this passage rather fitting, given what we're attempting...

- ❏ Read the section entitled **The Power of Teams** and give it careful consideration. The foundation you have been building these last few weeks is just the start of what God wants to do.

- ❏ Your memory verse this week is **Hebrews 6:11-12**. It is loaded with powerful words that highlight a number of critical points. Make sure you give each of these words the attention it deserves!

- ❏ This week's supplemental resource gives helpful suggestions for **Launching a Team**. If you don't feel quite ready to lead a FAST team on your own, determine to at least help out!

- ❏ We are on the downhill side of this course. It's time to double up on our prayers for revival, and to begin praying sincerely about what you will do after this course ends...

FAST
Forward Advancing Support Teams

Combustion Engines
Revival Keys > Week 7 > Bible Search

Topic: Deuteronomy 20:1-9

Brief Summary:

_____

_____

_____

_____

_____

_____

Observations/Insights:

_____

_____

_____

_____

_____

_____

Principles & Applications:

1. _____

   _____

   _____

2. _____

   _____

   _____

3. _____

   _____

   _____

4. _____

   _____

   _____

Main Point:

_____

_____

_____

_____

Combustion Engines
Revival Keys > Week 7 > Practical Suggestions

The Power of Teams

You are well on your way to becoming a Revival Agent. Your training is near complete. You know how to spark revival in your life through the internalization of God's Word. And you know how to lay a foundation for revival in your life through consistent discipleship: Bible study, prayer, personal obedience, and witnessing. And you have a strategy for revival that involves special revival meetings, combined with follow-up training. Stick to this strategy over time, and it will be sure to produce even more revival agents!

There's just one more thing to discuss: the power of teams.

You see, when it comes to revival, there's one thing you can know for sure: the enemy will be on hand to try and shut it down. Every time! There is nothing he fears more than that heaven will have some channel to pour its power through. So he will bring in accusations of emotionalism or fanaticism. He will provoke people to legalistic or imbalanced behavior. He will stir up controversy, or entice people down some theological rabbit hole. Or he'll simply lead people to question their experience, and doubt anything happened at all, until things dissipate into lethargy once again. I've seen all of this firsthand, and more.

In fact, your *MOST* vulnerable moment will likely be when this *Revival Keys* training comes to an end. When you and the other members of your team are confronted with the decision of what to do next...

By now you've surely tasted the power of a team to keep revival burning bright. There's something about the fellowship of committed Christians studying and praying together, setting goals and carrying them out, and doing ministry as a team—that keeps the flame hot. A group like this is a spiritual combustion engine. That band of commitment encircling a team like this, not only keeps its members close, but it keeps the enemy out too.

To keep your revival movement growing and advancing, it is important to continue meeting with the members of your team and/or others who share that same mission and purpose. In the paragraphs below, we will look at two specific reasons you should continue meeting together.

Continuing Education

First, ongoing training. Even though we are drawing near the end of this course, which is itself the third step in our three part discipleship curriculum, we've barely scratched the surface of the resources available to you. If you are serious about becoming a revival agent, continuing education is a must.

Our FAST ministry, for example, offers entire courses on pretty much every aspect of discipleship we've covered during our time together. We have a popular 30 day Breakout Memory Challenge which covers secrets to rapid verse accumulation that will electrify your internalization of Scripture. We also have whole courses on Bible study methods, principles of prayer, growing in obedience, personal witnessing, and more. We've covered the essentials during our time together, but there are huge amounts of additional information still ahead to deepen and reinforce your walk with God.

We also have an entire leadership track. It includes whole courses on how to transform churches into training centers, how to build effective outreach ministries, how to run evangelistic small groups, how to give Bible studies on important Bible topics, and even training in how to share God's endtime prophetic message. If you are serious about wanting to fulfill the Great Commission, then commit to investing whatever time it takes to get the training we need to become more effective. Which leads to the second thing your team can do together.

Strategic Planning

In addition to continuing education, your team should consider ongoing meetings to organize and coordinate your ministry as a team. You hopefully have lots of ideas about things you would like to do together as a result of the things you have studied. Conduct revival meetings. Organize training classes. Launch some community outreach, and more. You will be able to best accomplish these goals if you work together as a team.

As we've discussed before, good intentions need to be combined with strategic plans, with step by step objectives for accomplishing specific, shared goals. And no matter how good the plan, it won't accomplish anything without implementation! Every step needs to be carefully managed and executed. In addition, there needs to be constant evaluation, assessment, improvement. Consider incorporating the following kinds of activities into your weekly team meetings:

- Regularly review goals and priorities.
- Identify action items and "next-step" projects.
- Delegate tasks to specific team members.
- Set clear target dates and tracking progress.
- Share ministry reports and updates.
- Analyze results and refining plans.

By combining ongoing continuing education with ongoing strategic planning, your team will grow in both spirituality and impact.

The Future?

But it just gets better from there! In time your team will begin to grow in number too, as more people catch revival, are trained, and inspired for service. Soon, there may be enough to organize two or more teams. And that will produce even more benefits. By meeting at different times, more people will be able to find a team that fits their schedule. Different types of groups may develop—such as a mens group, or youth group. And different teams can focus on specific ministries—such as ministries to the homeless, or to college students. The greater the diversity of your teams, the easier it will be for each member of your church to find one that is right for them!

Of course, to keep things moving forward, each team must stay focused on the basics: memorization, discipleship and revival. The birth of each new team is an opportunity to review the core principles in the *Survival Kit*, *Basic Training*, and *Revival Keys*. And then continue on to whatever advanced training that group needs to achieve its ministry objectives. In time, revival may spread through your entire church. Even two or three teams, who stay faithful to the principles of revival, will be enough to spark surprising change. People will be coming to Christ through your outreach, and growing through your training. And from there, things will only accelerate.

Yes, the future is exciting. The possibilities are bright before you. But it all starts with that first team making the commitment to continue on...

Note: For more information about building your ministry leadership skills, check out our Leadership training track, at WWW.FAST.ST.

Combustion Engines
Revival Keys > Week 7 > Illustration

Launching a Team

Launching a new training team is always an exciting adventure! To be successful however, you cannot run it like a regular class or study group. Before launching your team we recommend reading our *Leaders Manual* at least twice and following its instructions closely. You should also be intimately familiar with the lessons you will be using. Make sure you understand how its content is organized, and the training objectives it is designed to achieve.

Here are a few additional steps to get your group started right:

- Spend some serious time in prayer, asking God to bless your efforts.
- Invite two or more individuals to be co-leaders with you. Having multiple leaders generally produces better training results. Plan your launch together.
- Discuss having a team with the appropriate leaders in your church. If possible, get a room during the weekly lesson study period of your church. If that's not possible choose another time and place.
- Ask God to impress just the right individuals to join your team. It is not the number that counts, but the commitment. So pray for a team that will give its best.
- Announce the launch date of the new team, and actively promote it through bulletin inserts, verbal announcements, posters in the foyer, etc. If you are doing revival meetings, promote it heavily as a follow up to those meetings.
- List names of specific individuals you would like to see in your team, and give each a personal invitation to join. Pray for them by name.
- Schedule your first meeting and remind everyone to be there on time. If your church is not a FAST training center, order the lessons early enough to get them in time. Otherwise, simply print them out.
- Plan the initial orientation meeting with your co-leaders, and launch your team. Congrats on getting off to a great start!

Walking Time Bombs

Week #8

Walking Time Bombs
Revival Keys > Week 8 > Memo

F
A
S
T

Memo:

Hard to believe, but we're almost to the end of this course. One lesson after this, and you'll be another graduate of *Revival Keys*! But don't think things are winding down. We've saved two of our best lessons for last!

This week we look at what being a graduate of this course really means. The potential of these simple concepts you have been learning, to transform your life. The wide open possibilities ahead, for your future. You may not sense anything is different, but you have changed.

You now have within you the DNA to ignite true revival. Anywhere in the world. At any time. Pursue what you've learned with all your heart and revival is sure to break out. The most exciting days of your life are just ahead.

**The Editor,
Hid in Christ**

Walking Time Bombs
Revival Keys > Week 8 >Objectives

Name: _____   Initialed by: _____

Date: _____

- ❏ For this week's Bible search, I want you to focus on **Matthew 10:1-42**. These are the instructions Jesus gave His disciples before sending them out. It's a bit long, so you'll only be able to skim the highlights, but it is worth the effort. Remember, these words were not just to them, but also to every future worker...

- ❏ Throughout these lessons, I've talked repeatedly about the need to become true **Agents of Revival**. This week we will be digging more into what that means. Ask God to give you even more of His Spirit as your work through this.

- ❏ Begin memorizing **Isaiah 49:6**. It is a bit long, but it is one of the most beautiful verses in the Bible. And definitely worth the effort! As you work on it, ask God to stretch your faith, and help you fully embrace what is promises.

- ❏ This week's supplemental resource is a quick **Discipleship Review**. Take a few moments to do an honest assessment of your life. Are there gaps in your walk with God? What can you do to correct those?

- ❏ You know the drill. Pray, pray, pray—for real revival. Revival for yourself. Revival for your team. Revival for your church. It may take time for God to work through the hindrances, but it can happen—if you believe.

FAST
Faithful, Available, Spiritual, Teachable

Walking Time Bombs
Revival Keys > Week 8 > Bible Search

Topic: Matthew 10:1-42

Brief Summary:

___

___

___

___

___

___

Observations/Insights:

___

___

___

___

___

___

Principles & Applications:

1. _____

   _____

   _____

2. _____

   _____

   _____

3. _____

   _____

   _____

4. _____

   _____

   _____

Main Point:

_____

_____

_____

_____

Walking Time Bombs
Revival Keys > Week 8 > Practical Suggestions

Agents of Revival
If you have made it this far in our *Revival Keys* course, you are ready to begin your ministry as a revival agent. You know our urgent need for revival. You know the essential conditions of revival: diligent study, earnest prayer, committed obedience, and sacrificial ministry. And you have the tools to put those things in place. You have a basic strategy to spark revival in your church, and to safeguard that experience. And you know the power of strong ministry teams to maintain momentum and ultimately transform your church. You may not feel all that different, but you've changed.

In this week's practical suggestions, we want to look at what it really means to be a revival agent. The possibilities ahead for your new life. The power of the training you have received. To do that, we want to start by looking at a most problematic passage...

A Perplexing Decision
Bible characters sometimes make decisions that seem strange to us, because we don't really understand their thinking. Take the decision Paul made in II Corinthians 2:12-13. In this passage, we see Paul entering a new city: Troas. And he goes there for a specific purpose: to preach the gospel. And when he arrives, something happens: a door opens for him. A door the Bible makes clear was opened for Paul by the Lord. Evidently the city was open to his message. The people were eager to receive his teaching. There was the potential for hundreds, perhaps thousands, to come to Christ!

But Paul finds himself balancing that opportunity with another pressing concern. Paul mentions how he had no rest in his spirit, because he didn't know what was happening with Titus, his friend and associate in ministry. On the one hand, he could stay in Troas and bring multitudes to salvation. Or he could leave it all behind, to go focus on one man who has already given his life to Christ. If you were faced with those options, which would you choose?

Many would focus on the city. But Paul says he left Troas, and went into Macedonia, evidently to look for Titus! He left a wide open opportunity for soul winning, to check up on one man. Why?

The Key Man Concept
We may never know the exact reason, but I believe it boiled down to training. Titus had spent years ministering together with Paul, and Paul knew that training had made Titus incredibly valuable to the cause of Christ.

Paul had no doubt invested heavily in Titus, passing on valuable knowledge, skills, vision. When commending Titus later in his letter to the Corinthians, Paul could say: "walked we not in the same spirit? walked we not in the same steps?" (II Corinthians 12:18). Much like he wrote of Timothy, Paul could count on Titus to bring those he taught "into remembrance of my ways which be in Christ, as I teach every where in every church" (I Corinthians 4:17). Essentially Paul had replicated himself in Titus. And in Timothy. And in others.

What was Paul's model of ministry? If you study his typical approach, you see he would go into a city, gather a group together, transform that church into a training center, and begin investing in people's lives. Soon revival would break out, and the Gospel would explode into the surrounding area. See Acts 19:8-10. It was pretty much what happened wherever Paul went. And no doubt the workers Paul trained followed that same exact strategy too.

Which explains why Paul chose Titus over Troas. Titus was not just one man, but the key to unlocking an entire city, an entire region. Titus was more important than Troas, because if Paul could somehow get him back into ministry, they could reach two cities, two regions. Paul wasn't looking at just one man, he was looking at the countless multitudes that one man could reach.

Training is what made Titus so valuable. He had become a key man. He had become a revival agent.

World Vision
The training you have received these last few months gives you similar value. If revival stays burning in your heart, you will have testimonies to share. And that will attract individuals, who are hungry to grow. And you know how to help them. At some point, you may be able to put together a team, and start training them systematically: in memorization, discipleship, and revival. And revival will soon be burning brightly in that new core group. Inevitably, it will spill out into your church. More teams will form. And as your church comes to life—it will spill out into your community. Soon you will be one of many, working and praising God together.

In time, it will spread to area churches. Some of those you train will move to other areas, and be able to spark revivals in those new churches. Perhaps you will be called to relocate for one reason or another, and have the privilege of being able to start the process all over, once again, somewhere else. From place to place, revival will spread. It can happen.

Why? Because you are that key man or woman God can use to unlock entire cities, entire regions. Because you are equipped to live as a revival agent.

At FAST, we believe world vision is seeing the world through one person. Seeing the potential of one person to multiply and become a thousand (Isaiah 60:22). Seeing that God has called each of us, to be His salvation "unto the end of the earth" (Isaiah 49:6). That is how we see you...

Truly, there's no limit to what God can do through one person who is willing to make room for the Holy Spirit to work through their life. Through one person willing to be a revival agent.

Note: For more information about becoming a spiritual leader, and maximizing all your spiritual faculties, check out our Moral Machinery study guides, by visiting us at WWW.FAST.ST.

Walking Time Bombs
Revival Keys > Week 8 > Illustration

Discipleship Review

Becoming a revival agent requires the foundation of a balanced life of discipleship. Here is a checklist of 28 suggested fundamental discipleship skills. Use it to make sure there are no missing pieces in your spiritual life:

- ❏ I have invited Jesus Christ to be my personal Lord and Savior.
- ❏ I am committed to making memorization on ongoing part of my life.
- ❏ I have set a minimum pace for how many verses to learn each week.
- ❏ I have a well organized review plan to ensure I retain memorized verses.
- ❏ I meet with a partner or group regularly for memorization accountability.
- ❏ I study the Bible daily, looking for principles that speak to me.
- ❏ I regularly connect the Word to my life through personal projects.
- ❏ I am able to do an inductive Bible study of a challenging passage.
- ❏ I keep an active prayer journal and pray through it faithfully.
- ❏ I connect specific Bible promises to my personal prayer requests.
- ❏ I record the dates I pray over my requests, and how I see God working.
- ❏ I know how to pray conversationally in a group.
- ❏ I actively use Scripture in my prayer life, and listen for God's voice.
- ❏ I use a master task list to track all the things I need to do.
- ❏ I make a to do list as part of my daily devotions and commit it to God.
- ❏ I have regular times to review my projects, plans, priorities, and purpose.
- ❏ I know how to use questions to exhort others to greater obedience.
- ❏ I have written out my personal testimony and can share it spontaneously.
- ❏ I can explain the gospel to another person using simple, clear language.
- ❏ I know the seven components of an unleashed outreach ministry.
- ❏ I have the basic skills necessary to help another believer grow spiritually.
- ❏ I believe training through teams maximizes spiritual growth.
- ❏ I see spiritual multiplication as God's plan for world evangelism.
- ❏ I believe revival is our greatest need, and pray for it daily.
- ❏ I know how to seek, spark and safeguard revival.
- ❏ I am committed to improving my life through continuing education.
- ❏ I am a part of a ministry team committed to seeking revival.
- ❏ I am personally determined to live as a revival agent in my church.

In Hot Pursuit

Week #9

In Hot Pursuit
Revival Keys > Week 9 > Memo

F
A
S
T

Memo:

Here it is, our final lesson. And perhaps our most challenging one yet! In it, we zoom in on earth's final revival. What we sometimes call the latter rain. That which will empower God's people to finish the work. To give the loud cry at last. Don't you long for that day?

Actually, it's what we've been talking about all along. It's not those "normal" revivals the church has enjoyed through the centuries that we want, but a different kind of revival. One built on solid biblical principles. One that endures and deepens rather than fizzling out. One that has the potential to spread everywhere. Until at long last the whole earth is gripped with its glory.

That revival is coming. And soon. Let's determine to work toward it intelligently—and be ready for it, when it comes...

**The Editor,
Hid in Christ**

In Hot Pursuit
Revival Keys > Week 9 > Objectives

Name: _____   Initialed by: _____

Date: _____

- ❑ Your final Bible Search is a deep one. **Matthew 25:1-13**. It's a familiar parable, but it merits more careful attention. What do the symbols all represent? What warning was Jesus trying to give. What does it tell you about earth's final revival?

- ❑ You are going to be excited about the title of our last practical suggestions: **The Latter Rain**. In it you'll find some vital parting insights into revival that are sure to thrill your heart...

- ❑ For your final memory verse this week, learn **Revelation 18:1**. It's a powerful prophecy, and it's fulfillment is just ahead for God's people. Come to the next team meeting prepared to quote it and all the verses you have been assigned so far. Determine to finish this course knowing every verse word-perfect!

- ❑ And one last time, we want to encourage you to pray for revival: for you, for your team, and for your church. And specifically to pray for the final revival. Unite your prayers with thousands of others around the world praying every day for the latter rain to come!

FAST
Finishing A Sacred Task

In Hot Pursuit
Revival Keys > Week 9 > Bible Search

Topic: Matthew 25:1-13

Brief Summary:

_____

_____

_____

_____

_____

_____

Observations/Insights:

_____

_____

_____

_____

_____

_____

Principles & Applications:

1. _____

   _____

   _____

2. _____

   _____

   _____

3. _____

   _____

   _____

4. _____

   _____

   _____

Main Point:

_____

_____

_____

_____

In Hot Pursuit
Revival Keys > Week 9 > Practical Suggestions

The Latter Rain
We have covered a lot as we've worked through the various lessons in this *Revival Keys* course. We've looked at our urgent need for revival, the key conditions for revival, how to spark revival, safeguard it, and see it spread. And we've encouraged you to see you potential as a revival agent. But this course is coming to a close, and we want to leave you with a few parting thoughts on revival. And in particular, earth's final revival. The latter rain.

You see, the history of the Christian church is sprinkled with genuine revivals all through the last 2000 years. Great spiritual awakenings, movements, outpourings of the Spirit. But they each have one thing in common: they have all come and gone. They burn brightly in some spot for a time, then fade away. They may spread a bit, or last a while—but inevitably they always fizzle out. These have all been early rain showers.

The final revival will be different. It starts somewhere, perhaps several places at once—but then keeps burning steadily. Rather than dissipating, it actually strengthens. And starts to spread. Here and there, little by little, from one place to another. Like a raging fire, it jumps every border, every boundary, every obstacle. It proves impossible to contain, and the whole world is engulfed at last. Until every nook and cranny of this world comes ablaze. Most will reject the blessing, but no one will escape its impact.

And even then, as probation starts to close, and God's people head into the final scenes of testing described in Revelation, this revival refuses to dim the least little bit, but rather, grows brighter and stronger still. In fact, it is this last outpouring that prepares God's people for the impending crisis.

The latter rain will be a global movement of unthinkable power. Earth's final revival will be unlike anything we've seen yet...

The Implications
All this suggests we are going to need to understand revival more fully. To participate in the latter rain, we are going to have to learn how to cooperate with God more completely. To grasp the dynamics of being Spirit-filled, Spirit-led, Spirit-empowered. We will have to become much more intelligent about what true revival is and how it works.

On the one hand we must know how to close and deadbolt the door against every kind of fanaticism. But on the other, we must learn how to give the Holy Spirit complete, unfettered access to our heart. We will need to understand how to discern a genuine experience, nurture it, cultivate it, deepen it, and ultimately, share it with others.

Some of these topics we've touched on in this *Revival Keys* course, but we've just dipped our toes into an ocean of deeper experience. Before God can trust us with the full endtime display of power He has promised, we are going to have to learn a lot more...

The Final Revival

FAST has been a revival-based ministry from it's very inception. And we've helped thousands experience a measure of revival through our various training resources. Not because there is anything special about our ministry, but because there is power in the Word of God. And we've stayed focused on giving people tools to connect to Scripture.

But through the years we've also reflected on this coming, final revival. On what the Latter Rain will be like. And we've gleaned a few insights along the way. Principles you too may find helpful. Here are a few quick ones:

It Won't Happen By Chance
Rather than happening spontaneously, the latter rain will be entered into deliberately, intentionally. God will have a people who understand the conditions for revival, and carefully prepare the way.

It Won't Be Mere Emotionalism
Many past revivals have been intensely emotional. The latter rain will be principled, firmly rooted in Scripture. It will be pursued calmly, and rationally.

It Won't Be Sensational
This kind of revival is not about outward show or external display. Rather, the latter rain leads to quiet repentance, and surrender to God. It creates deep internal change.

It Won't Lead to Extremism
While there will always be individuals who act in imbalanced ways, the latter rain brings people into order, unity, harmony. It draws people to a life of real biblical balance.

It Won't Chase New Light
Though great insights and discoveries are often made in times of revival, these never contradict or lead us away from established truth. Rather, the latter rain will cause us to focus more on applying Scripture to our life.

It Won't Attack God's Church
The church is the object of God's supreme regard. Critical attitudes stem from a lack of faith in God's power to revive and restore His church. The latter rain fills us with hope, in anticipation of a great awakening.

It Won't Make Us Arrogant
Instead of making us harsh or severe toward others, the latter rain will fill us with love for fellow believers, and make us humble, willing servants.

It Won't Neglect Evangelism
Rather than directing our energies toward other believers, the latter rain will compel us to reach out into our community, toward reaching lost souls for Christ. It gives power for finishing the work. And last...

It Won't Think Small
While we won't neglect personal or local revival, the latter rain is a global movement destined to impact the globe. We'll feel compelled to facilitate, coordinate, and support revival movements around the world.

No doubt there are many more lessons still to learn about revival. The closer we get to the end, the more we will understand how the Holy Spirit works. And the more intelligent we become, the more God can pour out His power.

One Final Thought

Here's one final thought. We can't keep putting the latter rain off to some distant time in the future. The Bible makes it clear, that when we reach the time in earth's history we need the latter rain, we are to ask for it (Zechariah 10:1). And that if we ask, God will give it. Not at some point in the future, not tomorrow, but today.

I believe that time is here. If you believe it too, won't you commit to praying for this great final outpouring of the Spirit of God? And to living YOUR life as a revival agent?

In Hot Pursuit
Revival Keys > Week 9 > Final Checklist

To finish this program, please verify completion of the following objectives:

Bible Searches
- ❏ Check here if you have done all nine Bible Searches

Practical Suggestions
- ❏ Conditions for Revival
- ❏ Searching the Word
- ❏ In Answer to Prayer
- ❏ Encouraging Exhortation
- ❏ A Heart for Ministry
- ❏ A Strategy for Revival
- ❏ The Power of Teams
- ❏ Agents of Revival
- ❏ The Latter Rain

Memory Verses
- ❏ Ephesians 5:14
- ❏ Psalms 119:18
- ❏ Proverbs 20:27
- ❏ Hebrews 3:13-14
- ❏ John 4:35
- ❏ Luke 11:13
- ❏ Hebrews 6:11-12
- ❏ Isaiah 49:6
- ❏ Revelation 18:1

Supplemental Resources
- ❏ Check here if you have read all eight Supplemental Resources

Congratulations! You have now completed FAST Revival Keys! We pray God has richly blessed your efforts to understand how God's Spirit works more fully. And we urge you to commit your life to becoming a revival agent!

Has this program been a blessing to you? Why not send us a note, and share how it has impacted your life? Thank you!

Additional Resources

From FAST

FAST Missions
Cutting-Edge Tools and Training

Ready to become a Revival Agent? FAST Missions can help! Our comprehensive training curriculum will give you the skills you need to take in God's Word effectively, live it out practically, and pass it on to others consistently.

Survival Kit
Eager to start memorizing God's Word? Our powerful keys will transform your ability to hide Scripture in your heart.

Basic Training
Want to explore the secrets of "real life" discipleship? Our next level training zooms in on critical keys to growth, like Bible study, prayer, time management, and more.

Revival Keys
Want to become a worker in the cause of Christ? Our most advanced training is designed to give you the exact ministry skills you need to see revival spread.

For more information, please visit us at:

WWW.FASTMISSIONS.COM

Study Guides

Looking for life-changing study guides to use in your small group or Bible study class? These resources have been used by thousands around the world. You could be next!

Survival Kit
Want to learn how to memorize Scripture effectively? These study guides will teach you 10 keys to memorization, all drawn straight from the Bible. Our most popular course ever!

Basic Training
Discover nuts and bolts keys to the core skills of discipleship: prayer, Bible study, time management, and more. Then learn how to share these skills with others. It is the course that launched our ministry!

Revival Keys
Now as never before, God's people need revival. And these guides can show you how to spark revival in your family, church, and community. A great revival is coming. Are you ready?

For more information about these and other study guides, please visit us at *http://fast.st/store*. Or look for these titles on Amazon.

Online Classes

Want to try out some of the resources available at FAST? Here is just a small sampling of courses from among dozens of personal and small group study resources:

Crash Course
Discover Bible-based keys to effective memorization. *http://fast.st/cc*

Fact or Fiction
Does the Bible really predict future events? You be the judge.
http://fast.st/prophecy

Monkey Business
Find out how evolution flunks the science test.
http://fast.st/monkey

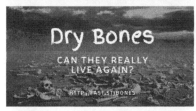

Dry Bones
Want more of God's Spirit? Learn how to pursue revival.
http://fast.st/bones

The Lost Art
Rediscover New Testament keys to making disciples.
http://fast.st/lostart

For more information about these and other classes, please visit us at *http://fast.st/classes*.

Digital Tools

FAST offers a number of powerful "apps for the soul" you can use to grow in your walk with God. And many of these are completely free to anyone with an account. Some of these include:

Review Engine
Our powerful review engine is designed to help ensure effective longterm Bible memorization. Give it a try, it works!

Bible Reading
An innovative Bible reading tool to help you read through the entire Bible, at your own pace, and in any order you want.

Prayer Journal
Use this tool to organize important requests, and we'll remind you to pray for them on the schedule you want.

Time Management
Learn how to be more productive, by keeping track of what you need to do and when. Just log in daily and get stuff done.

For more information about more than twenty tools like these, please visit us at *http://fast.st/tools*.

Books

If the content of this little book stirred your heart, look for these titles by the same author.

For Such A Time...
A challenging look at the importance of memorization for the last days, including topics such as the Three Angel's messages and the Latter Rain.

Moral Machinery
Discover how our spiritual, mental, and physical faculties work together using the sanctuary as a blueprint. Astonishing insights that could revolutionize your life!

The Movement
Discover God's plan to finish the work through a powerful endtime movement. Gain critical insights into what lies just ahead for the remnant!

For more information about these and other books, please visit us at *http://fast.st/store*. Or look for these titles on Amazon.

Made in United States
Troutdale, OR
01/02/2025